MW00913884

...*y encouraged*

by each other's faith.

ENCOURAGERS FOR MEN

ROMANS 1:12

FULFILLMENT
Living at Peace

Gary Wilde, ed.

VICTOR BOOKS

A DIVISION OF SCRIPTURE PRESS PUBLICATIONS INC.
USA CANADA ENGLAND

Scripture quotations are from the *Holy Bible, New International Version®*. Copyright © 1973, 1978, 1984 by International Bible Society. Used by permission of Zondervan Publishing House. All rights reserved.

Editors: Carolyn Nystrom & Greg Clouse
Designer: Andrea Boven
Cover Illustration: Mark Stearney
Cartoons: Rob Portlock

Recommended Dewey Decimal Classification: 248.832
Suggested Subject Heading: PERSONAL RELIGION, MEN

ISBN: 1-56476-515-6

1 2 3 4 5 6 7 8 9 10 Printing / Year 00 99 98 97 96

© 1996 by Victor Books / SP Publications, Inc.
All rights reserved. Printed in the United States of America.

TABLE OF CONTENTS

NOTES

Can you call back tomorrow?
Wednesdays are Mr. Bagley's doggy paddling day.

WELCOME TO...

An exciting men's study experience! Whether you'll be meeting with others in a group, or just going through this book on your own, you've made an excellent decision by choosing *Encouragers for Men.*

The volumes in this series are for men from every background and denomination, men who typically meet together to share their joys and hardships, their life concerns and prayer needs, their spiritual insights and questions – in short, to share their lives. Groups usually meet at lunch break or during an early morning breakfast. Or they may meet in a home during the evening.

According to a popular men's movement, our society views men as: mostly self-reliant, unable to feel or express emotion, unconcerned about fellowship, using people but loving things, primarily competitive, and too macho. You are taking an important step toward changing that description.

WHY THIS TOPIC?

Many men long for a group in which they can safely reveal their problems and receive the support they need to overcome them. Finding and befriending a fellow struggler brings tremendous encouragement, as men discover that they are not alone.

The book you've chosen, *Fulfillment: Living at Peace*, emphasizes the importance of this kind of fellowship for men who wish to explore daily living issues, such as:

- dealing with the "father-wound"
- handling unfulfilled dreams
- being the protector and rescuer
- finding ways to express emotions appropriately
- longing for security and settledness
- finding the balance between self-preservation and compassionate outreach

What happens when men do not find a group where this kind of sharing takes place? They may bog down in their spiritual journeys in one of two ways. First, some men continue seeking to control their circumstances. This stance characterizes the man who says, "I believe I should be joyful; I should feel fulfilled. But I never seem to reach it. I try and try, but something always goes wrong." When faced with dissatisfaction in life, he tries to force the circumstances to change so that he can once again feel happy. It doesn't work.

Second, some men keep trying to "act the part." This is almost the opposite approach. These are the guys who try to act as though things really are working out great all the time. Not content to savor the blessings and joys God sprinkles into their years, they may pretend unbroken daily bliss. In effect, they begin to fake the Christian life, wearing the mask of continual victory. And of course that doesn't work for long either.

The third and more truly Christian approach to life is left to those who are learning to embrace the pain – the pain and the struggle of spiritual pilgrimage. It's not the easy route to take, but it is the most honest. It brings us down to a basic reality, that everything we are and have is a product of the pure, unconditional grace of our Heavenly Father. And here's the key point: This approach to Christian living cannot be done in a vacuum. It requires fellowship, mutual encouragement, and ongoing accountability as men meet together to discuss their progress (successes and failures) along with their need for prayer. That is the way they help each other live for God, all along the way to Christian maturity.

How to Use This Guide

For Individual Use

Any man can benefit from personal study of the stories, Bible passages, quotes, and questions in this book. Just set aside a few minutes each day to be alone and in silence with your Lord. Ask Him to show you what you need to be learning about fellowship in His church. When you come to statements that refer to a group, creatively adapt them to your own relationship with God or with people that you know. Then try to put some of your insights into practical action.

For Use in a Men's Group

These sessions work great in a group of three to ten men. Make sure every man has a book, and use rotating leadership each week. Participants should try to come to the session having read the chapter. But for those who come unprepared, the chapters are short enough to skim or read aloud during the group time itself. The key to the study format is simply "laying material out on the table" for discussion. Men will pick up on this and feel free to let the discussion move into their particular areas of concern.

Preparing to Lead a Group Session

See the *Can You Relate?* section of each session for your basic outline as you take your turn leading discussion in the group. When it's your turn to lead, your job is to act as a discussion facilitator, not a teacher. Before the session you'll spend some time thinking about how the readings relate to your own journey of spiritual growth. Answer the three questions below, and you will have all the material you need for generating discussion—because people will feel free to contribute their own insights, comments, and questions in response. (You will also find specific questions about your particular topic in the section, *For Further Thought or Discussion.*)

- ▸ What experience in my own life confirms (or disputes) the material I've read?
- ▸ What themes or statements stand out to me as most important, significant, or controversial?
- ▸ What questions, comments, insights, or personal applications flow from this material?

Getting a Handle on the Format

Here are some explanations of the items you'll find in each *Encouragers* chapter. Items 2, 3, and 4 below provide the overall theme for discussion. Group members will choose the parts of these story-sections that strike them as significant, and they'll relate those stories to their own experience. The goal is personal application, in the context of group accountability, for the purpose of solid spiritual growth.

▶ 1. *Check-in/Update.* Sessions typically open with each group member "reporting in." Sharing consists of "I" statements about life as it is at the moment: A feeling to report, a problem to share, a personal or spiritual growth question or insight, a summary of the week, a progress/accountability check.

▶ 2. *One Man's Story.* This opening vignette offers one man's experience with the topic. It is a personal, "how-I-see-this-issue" report, intended to put the subject into the context of everyday life.

▶ 3. *God Enters the Story.* These are printed Scripture passages related to the topic—there for your reference. Some groups will focus heavily here; others will simply let the Scripture serve as a theological boundary for the discussion. The fact is that "our story" (the way we actually live) often clashes with God's story (the call to deeper commitment and holiness). This creates a tension that makes for excellent discussion: How can God's story become, to a greater degree, the story of our own Christian growth?

▶ 4. *The Story in Quotes.* These brief excerpts add spice to your discussion. They are sometimes profound insights, sometimes controversial thought-starters. Some group members will agree with the statements, others may disagree. The quotes are often drawn from the devotional classics, but can come from any source, secular or religious.

▶ 5. *Can You Relate?* You'll find a set of four general questions in each session. The leader uses these questions to make up the basic "plan" of the session time. Sometimes your group will go no further than responding to these questions.

▶ 6. *For Further Thought or Discussion.* Here you will find creative ways to explore the issues raised in this particular chapter.

▶ 7. *Prayer Moments.* Your group members will choose, each week, how to use their prayer time. Varying the approach gives each group member a chance to pray in a way that is most comfortable.

▶ 8. *Suggestion for the Week Ahead.* Here you're given practical life-response suggestions related to the week's topic. You may wish to use these suggestions to set up an ongoing accountability report to be given during each session. This is a way of inviting each other to check up on your progress. Each group member can choose suggestions that will help him take the first steps toward change.

▶ 8. *The "Back Pages" Resources.* Be sure to check out the *Group Strengtheners* provided in the back pages of this book. You'll find: *Creative Session Starters,* a *Fellowship Day Idea Starter,* a *Video Night Discussion Outline,* and a *Prayer Record.*

So, ready to begin? Call the men, set a time and a place for your weekly meetings, and get started!

Healing the Father-Wound

What's happening with you?

- ► A feeling to report
- ► A problem to share
- ► A personal or spiritual growth question or insight
- ► A summary of your week: issues, concerns, and joys
- ► A progress report or accountability check

► **ONE MAN'S STORY**

We buried Dad, Major Amos E. Simmons (Ret.), in the family cemetery by a country road about one-half mile from where he was born and raised. The soldiers came from Ft. Polk, draped an American flag over his silver-blue casket, and saluted him with rifle fire. A solitary trooper played taps on his bugle. We prayed. I cried.

I cried because I had loved him for only three years. I had hated him for twenty-five years and had liked him for eight years. I felt cheated. I wanted my dad back. We were busy building good memories to replace the painful ones. . . .

He was a powerful man: tall, stiff-backed, with ice blue eyes and prematurely snow-white hair. He was the arm wrestling champ of several army bases. But he had doubts about his ability to raise a son. I now understand why. His father, "ole man" Luther, had the awesome job of keeping the family of nine children together during the depression without a wife. Dad's mother died when he was four years old. Times were tough, men were tough, and they weren't soft on kids. My grandfather once ran a 1927 Ford Model T touring car into the back of one of his logging trucks and tore the radiator loose. He drove it home anyway, parked it, got an ax, and chopped it to pieces. That was the way he did things, and that was the way he raised kids. . . .

With a track record of fathering like this one in his blood, no wonder Dad was worried about how he was going to raise me. . . . To make me tough, he would walk me out to the playground and actually pick fights for me. I remember once in Berlin, Germany, Dad looked out the window and saw three German boys walking by our house. He ran over, threw open the door, and said, "Get out there and whip those boys, and if you don't, I'm going to whip you."

I seethed with bitterness and rebellion toward Dad. I could not confront him openly (I tried once and he broke my nose), so I struck back in sneaky ways that I couldn't get caught and punished for. I deliberately sabotaged things and failed at things just to watch him blow up. I withheld the only things Dad needed from me: love and respect. . . .

But I didn't leave Dad behind when I left home, and he didn't leave me behind when he died. Our fathers never leave us. They hang around in our minds for the rest of our lives, and their voices keep repeating all the things we heard as we grew up.

—Dave Simmons[1]

▶ GOD ENTERS THE STORY

The next day, the second day of the month, David's place was empty again. Then Saul said to his son Jonathan, "Why hasn't the son of Jesse come to the meal, either yesterday or today?"

Jonathan answered, "David earnestly asked me for permission to go to Bethlehem. He said, 'Let me go, because our family is observing a sacrifice in the town and my brother has ordered me to be there. If I have found favor in your eyes, let me get away to see my brothers.' That is why he has not come to the king's table."

Saul's anger flared up at Jonathan and he said to him, "You son of a perverse and rebellious woman! Don't I know that you have sided with the son of Jesse to your own shame and to the shame of the mother who bore you? As long as the son of Jesse lives on this earth, neither you nor your kingdom will be established. Now send and bring him to me, for he must die!"

"Why should he be put to death? What has he done?" Jonathan asked his father. But Saul hurled his spear at him to kill him. Then Jonathan knew that his father intended to kill David. Jonathan got up from the table in fierce anger; on that second day of the month he did not eat, because he was grieved at his father's shameful treatment of David.

—1 Samuel 20:27b-34

"Why does the son not share the guilt of his father?" Since the son has done what is just and right and has been careful to keep all my decrees, he will surely live. The soul who sins is the one who will die. The son will not share the guilt of the father, nor will the father share the guilt of the son. The righteousness of the righteous man will be credited to him, and the wickedness of the wicked will be charged against him.

—*Ezekiel 18:19-20*

Our fathers disciplined us for a little while as they thought best; but God disciplines us for our good, that we may share in His holiness.

—*Hebrews 12:10*

▶ THE STORY IN QUOTES

It was surprising to me when almost a decade ago I realized I had within me a wound, a source of weakness, shame, codependence, and grief, that I had received at the hands of my father. I was also surprised to find that, in order to move forward into a fulfilling life, I had to recover from that wound.

—Michael Gurian[2]

More than anything else in the world I wanted my father to love me, just like I loved him. The Beatles sang "All You Need Is Love"—and that was all I wanted from Dad. It's difficult to explain why I should feel so strongly when we shared so little. Never once in all the years he lived in America did he even think about coming to see me. Apart from rare visits, I lived from birthdays to Christmas just to hear from him. Yet if anyone suggests Dad wasn't quite perfect, I find myself justifying him. I've only recently begun to admit he was not the perfect father, not even the perfect man. Yet I can't let go. I think of him almost all the time.

—Julian Lennon, son of John Lennon[3]

It's a wonderful thing when your father becomes not a god but a man to you—when he comes down from the mountain and you see he's this man with weaknesses. And you love him as this whole being, not as a figurehead.

—Robin Williams[4]

▶ **CAN YOU RELATE?**

▶ Which one of the three story-sections above "rang a bell" with you? How?

▶ What personal story or experience comes to mind, in relation to the theme of carrying a wound from your father?

▶ What other insights came to the surface for you? What questions were raised in your mind? What personal applications are you considering?

▶ What else would you like to say about this topic?

▶ **FOR FURTHER THOUGHT OR DISCUSSION**

▶ Can you recall times when your father acted as Saul did—shamefully? If so, how has that affected you?

▶ What forms of reconciliation with your father have you experienced—or at least tried to bring about?

▸ Meditate on Ezekiel 18:19-20 for a moment. What does it take for a man to break free of any guilt he may be carrying that really belongs to his father? Relate your response to the message of the Gospel.

▸ See Hebrews 12:10. In what ways is an earthly father's discipline less than perfect, compared to the Heavenly Father's discipline? How have you experienced these differences in your own life?

▸ See the quote by Robin Williams. When did your own father "come down from the mountain"? What did this mean for you, in practical terms? How did it change your relationship?

▸ PRAYER MOMENTS

Spend some time going around the circle, naming specific prayer needs. Use the Prayer Record *on page 62 to jot notes. Then, choose a prayer method below:*

___ One man prays, covering issues and concerns raised.

___ Everyone prays for the man on his right.

___ Pray sentence prayers, with a person designated to close.

___ Focus on one key concern of the group or a group member, and all pray about that concern.

___ Spend some moments in silent prayer.

___ Assign specific prayer subjects to people before bowing for prayer.

___ Lay hands on a brother who expresses need, and focus on that man's situation.

___ Sing the doxology, or a praise chorus.

___ Other method:

▶ **SUGGESTION FOR THE WEEK AHEAD**

In the coming week, make some time to think about any wounds you are still carrying from your relationship with your father—whether he is still living, or not. Then develop a "recovery prescription" for yourself. First, jot descriptions or examples of your symptoms. Then, prescribe some practical steps to take toward your healing. Consider using the two columns below on a separate sheet of paper:

SYMPTOMS   PRESCRIPTION

▸ anger in my life
   (describe):

▸ shame in my life
   (describe):

▸ guilt in my life
   (describe):

▸ grief in my life
   (describe):

▸ other
   (describe):

Dreaming of the Future

What's happening with you?

- A feeling to report
- A problem to share
- A personal or spiritual growth question or insight
- A summary of your week: issues, concerns, and joys
- A progress report or accountability check

▶ ONE MAN'S STORY

I was to be the next Billy Graham—so I thought as a teenager. Amazingly, thirty years later I discovered the guy working at a desk job in the cubicle next to me had also expected to be the future Billy Graham. I then pondered how many Billy Grahams-to-be grew up during the 1950s.

Later I matured. I was to be a seminary professor. People told me so. I even have a Ph.D., so I'm ready. To compound my frustrations, there are three guys from my graduating class who are presidents of Christian colleges or seminaries. Two of those same three once recommended me for honors or positions I never received. And the third—nobody in our class ever would have picked him as the president of . . . well, I won't name it. Now that I've passed the half-century mark, I'm still wondering what I'm going to be when I grow up!

Charles Dickens wrote *Great Expectations*. I think I'm a victim of Christian literature's too-great expectations. I read how Charles Finney would step into a room and sinners would be smitten with conviction by the Spirit. I had great expectations, but I seemed to be a bystander alongside the parade of life.

My dreams didn't include sitting at a desk evaluating oh-so-thrilling nursery-level Sunday School curriculum. When midlife crisis got me depressed, a counselor indicated I needed to come to terms with life's three A's: (1) Accept; (2) Adapt; or (3) Alter.

ACCEPT life. Just as it is. Just as I am. Who am I to say to the divine Potter (á la Romans 9:20): "How come I'm where I am?" I have a great wife. I have wonderful friends. I have ministry opportunities. Jesus spent ten-elevenths of His life not doing "ministry."

ADAPT. If my dream was to be a seminary professor, why can't I perform the same function with whatever people God gives me to lead and teach? My dream can be modified to fit my personal circumstances.

ALTER. Perhaps I'm too laid back about achieving my aims. Do I need to send out more resumés? (After all, they say that's the way many jobs come.) Do I expect God just to drop my dreamworld job on my head, or shall I say with Paul, "I labor, struggling with all His energy"? (Colossians 1:29, NIV)

"I know not what the future holds, but I know who holds the future" says a song. Can I learn to say with Paul, "I have learned the secret of being content in any and every situation"?

—Jim Townsend

He hasn't been the same since Joe Montana retired.

 ▶ GOD ENTERS THE STORY

Now this is what the Lord Almighty says: "Give careful thought to your ways.

You have planted much, but have harvested little. You eat, but never have enough. You drink, but never have your fill. You put on clothes, but are not warm. You earn wages, only to put them in a purse with holes in it."

This is what the Lord Almighty says: "Give careful thought to your ways. Go up into the mountains and bring down timber and build the house, so that I may take pleasure in it and be honored," says the Lord.

"You expected much, but see, it turned out to be little. What you brought home, I blew away. Why?" declares the Lord Almighty. "Because of my house, which remains a ruin, while each of you is busy with his own house. Therefore, because of you the heavens have withheld their dew and the earth its crops. I called for a drought on the fields and the mountains, on the grain, the new wine, the oil and whatever the ground produces, on men and cattle, and on the labor of your hands."

—*Haggai 1:5-11*

"For I know the plans I have for you," declares the Lord, "plans to prosper you and not to harm you, plans to give you hope and a future."

—*Jeremiah 29:11*

But seek first His kingdom and His righteousness, and all these things will be given to you as well.

—*Matthew 6:33*

 ▶ **THE STORY IN QUOTES**

Ever reach a point in your life where you say, "This is the best I'm ever going

to look, ever going to feel, ever going to do . . . and it ain't that great"?
— Billy Crystal, as Mitch, in the movie *City Slickers*[5]

The trouble about reaching the age of ninety-two, which I did last October, is that regrets for a misspent life are bound to creep in, and whenever you see me with a furrowed brow you can be sure that what is on my mind is the thought that if only I had taken up golf earlier and devoted my whole time to it instead of fooling about writing stories and things, I might have got my handicap down to under eighteen.
— P.G. Wodehouse[6]

He was one of those men who struggle for success long after they have it, who are still making touchdowns when the stands are empty, the other team long gone, and the shadows lengthening toward them. Like most of us, he was seeking happiness, and was baffled that success had not brought it. But success itself is a sort of failure. You reach the end of the rainbow, and there's no pot of gold. You get your castle in Spain, and there's no plumbing.
— Charlie Brower[7]

▶ CAN YOU RELATE?

▶ Which one of the three story-sections above "rang a bell" with you? How?

▶ What personal story or experience comes to mind, in relation to these themes:

(a) handling unfulfilled dreams

(b) wanting more out of life

▸ What other insights came to the surface for you? What questions were raised in your mind? What personal applications are you considering?

▸ What else would you like to say about this topic?

▸ **FOR FURTHER THOUGHT OR DISCUSSION**

▸ On a scale of 1 to 5, how would you rate yourself:

1	2	3	4	5
All of my dreams are coming to pass				My dreams never seem to work out

▸ How were you taught, perhaps as a boy, to "stand still," to be a good scout, to not get so excited? How does this early-and-often command clash with your desire to pursue your dreams at full speed?

▸ Look again at *One Man's Story.* Have you ever felt like you were on hold, just treading water, "a bystander alongside the parade of life," as Jim Townsend describes? How have you dealt with that?

▸ The message of the Prophet Haggai includes a description of the consequences of improper priorities. How do kingdom priorities fit in with your current dreams and goals?

▸ What does Charlie Brower mean when he says that success itself is a sort of failure?

▸ How do you, personally, define success?

▸ **PRAYER MOMENTS**

Spend some time going around the circle, naming specific prayer needs. Use the Prayer

Record *on page 62 to jot notes. Then, choose a prayer method below.*

__ One man prays, covering issues and concerns raised.

__ Everyone prays for the man on his right.

__ Pray sentence prayers, with a person designated to close.

__ Focus on one key concern of the group or a group member, and all pray about that concern.

__ Spend some moments in silent prayer.

__ Assign specific prayer subjects to people before bowing for prayer.

__ Lay hands on a brother who expresses need, and focus on that man's situation.

__ Sing the doxology, or a praise chorus.

__ Other method:

▶ SUGGESTION FOR THE WEEK AHEAD

Think about your priorities this week—and compare your stated priorities to your priorities as lived.

First, jot a "Top Ten" list of your priorities on a sheet of paper. Then write some goals that you have had in the past and that you have for the present and the future.

Ask yourself: *To what extent do my stated priorities seem to influence my actual goals and actions? In light of the way I'm living my life, what appear to be my real priorities?*

Playing the Rescuer

What's happening with you?

- ▶ A feeling to report
- ▶ A problem to share
- ▶ A personal or spiritual growth question or insight
- ▶ A summary of your week: issues, concerns, and joys
- ▶ A progress report or accountability check

▶ ONE MAN'S STORY

Once again we'd fallen into the same old verbal spiral, a marital battle that escalated along well-worn paths of pain and confusion. Here's how it goes: She's being mistreated at work. I listen for a while, telling myself that this time I will only play the role of comforter and encourager. But the reports of unfairness and apparent injustice light my fuse. I get angry and want to protect her and defend her; I'll do anything to fix her problem and make her life all right again. But, once again, she interprets the anger as being directed at her. *No! You don't understand; I'm just angry about what's happening to you. . . .*

Deep inside I know that all she wants is a listening ear and a little comfort. But I feel wired to protect, driven to solve her problem: "You should have said *this*; you could have done *that*."

Why can't I let her have her own life? Isn't she allowed to have problems and struggles too, just like me? I've grown through facing adversity, haven't I? Why can't I allow my wife the same privilege? Besides, who made me responsible to make everything okay, anyway?

Somehow, for me, it all connects back to the day of my father's funeral when, as we slowly followed the casket into the church, I took my grandfather's words deeply to heart as *The Truth* of my life: "Get up there and take care of your mother. You're the man of the house now."

A man is taught to be a problem-solver, a helper, a fixer, a hero, a rescuer of women. But does playing this role require the other person to be in the role of the problem, the help-ee, the broken, the vanquished, the wounded? Is that really where our wives ought to be?

Truth to tell, I enjoy being the "knight in shining armor." And there's surely a legitimate place for manly leadership and protection. But suppose this role-playing were gradually transformed a bit. Maybe some new lines of honest communication might open—if I can release myself from the hero-role and step off the pedestal.

—Gary Wilde

 ▶ **GOD ENTERS THE STORY**

Then Samson's wife [a woman from Timnah] threw herself on him, sobbing,

"You hate me! You don't really love me."
—*Judges 14:16a*

Then [Delilah] said to him, "How can you say, 'I love you,' when you won't confide in me? This is the third time you have made a fool of me and haven't told me the secret of your great strength." With such nagging she prodded him day after day until he was tired to death.

So he told her everything. . . . Having put him to sleep on her lap, she called a man to shave off the seven braids of his hair, and so began to subdue him. And his strength left him.
—*Judges 16:15, 17, 19*

[Ruth] exclaimed, "Why have I found such favor in your eyes that you notice me—a foreigner?"

Boaz replied, "I've been told all about what you have done for your mother-in-law since the death of your husband—how you left your father and mother and your homeland and came to live with a people you did not know before. May the Lord repay you for what you have done. May you be richly rewarded by the Lord, the God of Israel, under whose wings you have come to take refuge."

"May I continue to find favor in your eyes, my lord," she said. "You have given me comfort and have spoken kindly to your servant—though I do not have the standing of one of your servant girls."

At mealtime Boaz said to her, "Come over here. Have some bread and dip it in the wine vinegar." When she sat down with the harvesters, he offered her some roasted grain. She ate all she wanted and had some left over. As she got up to glean, Boaz gave orders to his men, "Even if she gathers among the sheaves, don't embarrass her. Rather, pull out some stalks for her from the bundles and leave them for her to pick up, and don't rebuke her. . . .

And now, my daughter, don't be afraid. I will do for you all you ask."

— *Ruth 2:10-16; 3:11*

▶ THE STORY IN QUOTES

Men are like that. We cast others, especially women, in follower roles, because we are cast in leader roles. Then we coach them to be good followers and diagnose bad following as a problem. Neither of us wants this when we stop to think about it. But the casting is as though in bronze. . . . To be a man, I must control or manage or help, so I search out and create people to control or manage or help, often women. Men are taught that high stakes are attached to bossing or helping or completing a woman.

— James E. Dittes[8]

Years ago, manhood was an opportunity for achievement, and now it is a problem to be overcome. Plato, St. Francis, Michelangelo, Mozart, Leonardo da Vinci, Vince Lombardi, Van Gogh — you don't find guys of that caliber today, and if there are any, they are not painting the ceiling of the Sistine Chapel or composing *Don Giovanni*. They are trying to be Mr. O.K. All-Rite, the man who can bake a cherry pie, go play basketball, come home, make melon balls and whip up a great soufflé, converse easily about intimate matters, participate in recreational weeping, laugh, hug, be vulnerable, be passionate in a skillful way, and the next day go off and lift them bales into that barge and tote it. A guy who women consider Acceptable.

Being all-rite is a dismal way to spend your life, and guys are not equipped for it anyway. We are lovers and artists and adventurers, meant to be noble, free-ranging, and foolish, like dogs, not competing for a stamp of approval: "Friend of Womanhood."

—Garrison Keillor[9]

▶ CAN YOU RELATE?

▶ Which one of the three story-sections above "rang a bell" with you? How?

▶ What personal story or experience comes to mind, in relation to these themes:

(a) being the protector and rescuer

(b) feeling responsible for another's happiness

▶ What other insights came to the surface for you? What questions were raised in your mind? What personal applications are you considering?

▶ What else would you like to say about this topic?

▶ FOR FURTHER THOUGHT OR DISCUSSION

▶ In the story of Samson, what were the two women wanting from Samson? What methods did they use? Have such methods ever been used with you?

▶ Have you ever felt, like Samson, that you had to give your strength to a woman in order to please her?

▶ In the story of Ruth, what might be some of the effects of making the kind of promise that Boaz makes in Ruth 3:11?

▸ As a professional, or as a spouse, have you ever been "set up" to play a role that you never asked for? What happened?

▸ Where do you draw the line between legitimate helping or leading and inappropriate rescuing? Can you give an example?

▸ PRAYER MOMENTS

Spend some time going around the circle, naming specific prayer needs. Use the Prayer Record *on page 62 to jot notes. Then, choose a prayer method below.*

__ One man prays, covering issues and concerns raised.

__ Everyone prays for the man on his right.

__ Pray sentence prayers, with a person designated to close.

__ Focus on one key concern of the group or a group member, and all pray about that concern.

__ Spend some moments in silent prayer.

__ Assign specific prayer subjects to people before bowing for prayer.

__ Lay hands on a brother who expresses need, and focus on that man's situation.

__ Sing the doxology, or a praise chorus.

__ Other method:

▸ SUGGESTION FOR THE WEEK AHEAD

Do some thinking about these questions during the week: In what specific situations is it legitimate for me to be the "knight in shining armor"—hero, protector, rescuer? And when does playing that role place others among the vanquished?

Use columns like these to aid your thought process:

Times for knighthood	Times to remove the armor
► When . . .	When . . .
► When . . .	When . . .
► When . . .	When . . .

SESSION 4

Pursuing Emotional Wholeness

CHECK-IN / UPDATE

What's happening with you?

- A feeling to report
- A problem to share
- A personal or spiritual growth question or insight
- A summary of your week: issues, concerns, and joys
- A progress report or accountability check

▶ ONE MAN'S STORY

By the age of thirty-two, I had achieved what I thought was best: I was married, had three children, and served as the director of a social services agency with over seventy-five employees. Then one day, I woke up on a cold winter morning depressed and not wanting to get out of bed. I couldn't think, pray, or act my way through it. I was stuck; I didn't even know what to feel.

You see, the subject of emotions was never talked about by anyone as I was growing up. Dogma was taught, morality was preached, but no one ever directly talked about their own feelings or took an interest in my emotional life.

I did get edicts regarding emotions, of course—from parents, church, school, and culture:

"Crying only makes things worse."
"Talking back is disrespectful."
"There's nothing to be afraid of."
"Stop your crying or I'll give you something to cry about."
"Christians shouldn't get angry."
"Don't feel bad; with God, you are never alone."
"Lusting after women is sinful, you know."

Consequently, with the combination of negative messages regarding emotions and the nonexistence of anyone explaining to me the emotional aspects of life, I came into adulthood almost totally emotionally repressed. My intellect had been honed through having heard that I had "a good head on my shoulders," that I should "use my head," "keep my head on straight," "get ahead," and "think before I act." But my emotions were nonexistent, kept tightly controlled by my rational mind and my church behavior. When circumstances occasionally provoked a bubbling of emotions to the surface, I was either unaware, embarrassed, or felt guilty.

Finally, a few days after I had "shut down" on that cold morning, I picked up a book by Christian psychologist, Dr. Cecil Osborne, and read about a process for healing depression. I called him, scheduled an appointment, and took two weeks off from home and work responsibilities to see if he could help me.

During my time in therapy, I learned about the emotional life and went through a process in which

I could experience the range of emotions I had walled up so deep inside me: the terror from emotional and physical abuse; the sadness of my father's death when I was seventeen; the loneliness of my marriage and job; the rage at having had to keep all my feelings inside me. During this time too, I had a powerful dream in which it seemed that my father came to me. In the dream, he told me he was sorry for never letting me express my

For $2.00 you get a hug with it.

emotions to him. He then said to me: "You never have to apologize for what you feel, ever again."

Thanks to the healing that came through counseling and this unusual dream-blessing, I have been able to experience and celebrate my emotional life and the energy and information it brings me. And since that day, I have never experienced depression.

—Samuel Prentice, Jr.

▶ GOD ENTERS THE STORY

[Jesus] withdrew about a stone's throw beyond them, knelt down and prayed, "Father, if You are willing, take this cup from Me; yet not My will, but Yours be done."

An angel from heaven appeared to Him and strengthened Him. And being in anguish, He prayed more earnestly, and His sweat was like drops of blood falling to the ground.

—Luke 22:41-44

Jesus wept.

—John 11:35

When it was almost time for the Jewish Passover, Jesus went up to Jerusalem. In the temple courts He found men selling cattle, sheep and doves, and others sitting at tables exchanging money. So He made a whip out of cords, and drove all from the temple area, both sheep and cattle; He scattered the coins of the money changers and overturned their tables.

To those who sold doves He said, "Get these out of here! How dare you turn My Father's house into a market!"

—John 2:13-16

Your attitude should be the same as that of Christ Jesus.
—*Philippians 2:5*

▶ THE STORY IN QUOTES

Jesus didn't suppress His anger any more than He exploded with rage that day in the temple. His anger was up front, out in the open. He responded to the situation quickly, positively and appropriately, then went on with His business.

If a man buries his anger inside, he's only storing up pressure for a later implosion (hurting himself) and/or explosion (hurting others). If he doesn't bring his anger to the surface and deal with it, someday, somewhere, somehow it will express itself in an out-of-bounds manner, and somebody will get hurt.
—Stephen Arterburn and David Stoop[10]

Every unfelt feeling is a prism through which we see life in a distorted way.
—Cecil Osborne[11]

I have heard person after person at men's conferences testify that they grew up without any model of what an activated masculine emotional body is. Some men describe scenes in childhood in which the mother flew into a rage, directed at the father or at men in general, and their father said nothing, sank into silence and guilt, or disappeared from the room, having defended neither himself nor the boy. Others have known only robotlike fathers, or victim fathers without a job, or playboy fathers without depth. The man without an activated emotional body may alternate between abusive behavior and impotent gentleness that isn't really gentle.

—Robert Bly[12]

▶ CAN YOU RELATE?

▸ Which one of the three story-sections above "rang a bell" with you? How?

▸ What personal story or experience comes to mind, in relation to these themes:

(a) squelching emotions growing up

(b) finding ways to express emotions appropriately as an adult

▸ What other insights came to the surface for you? What questions were raised in your mind? What personal applications are you considering?

▸ What else would you like to say about this topic?

▶ FOR FURTHER THOUGHT OR DISCUSSION

▸ Is Samuel's "success story" with depression a realistic possibility for everyone? Why or why not?

▸ In your opinion, what is the role of counseling, or psychotherapy, in the Christian life?

▸ What kinds of emotions did Jesus experience in the Scripture passages printed above?

▸ What other examples from Scripture show Jesus expressing strong feeling?

▸ For a moment, imagine being Jesus. You are gathering the cords and putting the whip together, just before chasing people out of the temple courts (see John 2:15). How are you feeling at that moment?

► Many men experience their emotions primarily in muscle tension, headaches, self-shaming thoughts, outbursts of rage, or other physical and mental symptoms. Why do you think this is the case?

► Do you believe that a man's rage or depression shows that he has "stuffed" his feelings? If so, what steps can a man take to change?

► PRAYER MOMENTS

Spend some time going around the circle, naming specific prayer needs. Use the Prayer Record *on page 62 to jot notes. Then, choose a prayer method below:*

__ One man prays, covering issues and concerns raised.

__ Everyone prays for the man on his right.

__ Pray sentence prayers, with a person designated to close.

__ Focus on one key concern of the group or a group member, and all pray about that concern.

__ Spend some moments in silent prayer.

__ Assign specific prayer subjects to people before bowing for prayer.

__ Lay hands on a brother who expresses need, and focus on that man's situation.

__ Sing the doxology, or a praise chorus.

► SUGGESTION FOR THE WEEK AHEAD

*D*o some thinking this week along these lines: *How do I know when I am sad? angry? fearful? joyful?*

- ► How my body feels at those times:

- ► How my mind works at those times:

- ► How I act at those times:

Ask yourself: *Do I experience a wide range of emotions? Or do they all seem to merge into just one general feeling (for example, all my emotions are felt as: shame, rage, fear, nervousness, other)?*

Wanting to Be Settled

What's happening with you?

- A feeling to report
- A problem to share
- A personal or spiritual growth question or insight
- A summary of your week: issues, concerns, and joys
- A progress report or accountability check

► ONE MAN'S STORY

I lived in Chicago, right downtown, and life was often hectic, fast-paced, and draining. So it made sense that this kind of question would surface in my mind, as I drove back from a trip in the country: *Is it possible in this life just to be content — just to live, without all the striving and struggling?*

I was headed back to the Windy City, driving through miles and miles of cornfields in southern Illinois, passing through the tiniest of small towns, one by one, separated by long stretches of flat, state-road pavement. Everything about those little towns looked blissfully settled, peaceful, and serene. Each quaint community, with its couple of white steepled churches, its inevitable grain elevator, its rows of clapboard houses with perfectly manicured lawns and flower beds, spoke to me of a heavenly existence, far from the cacophony of the subway tracks and blaring sirens that would soon envelop me once again. Surely these were places where a man and his family could live out their days in peace and warmth and love.

Boy, imagine living in a place like this: Get up in the morning, go to work—in the fields or at the feed store—come home, play with the kids, sit in the lawn chair, watch the sun go down, and go to bed in peace. We're talking hassle-free living here, far from the rat race. Wow!

But, of course, it was all a fantasy—pleasant and compelling—but a fantasy nonetheless. For I knew that each picket-fenced yard harbored a house where real people lived, with all of their unique problems and struggles. If I could exchange my hectic pace for their seemingly tranquil existence, perhaps I would. But I know I'd just be inheriting a brand new set of problems too. There's no escape from that.

But is it wrong to seek contentment? Perhaps not, if I learn to give thanks that, when it comes, it is always temporary, a fleeting preview to a better existence. For this is not yet Home—no matter how hard I try to make it so. There will always be a steep relational mountain to climb, a gut-wrenching trial to face, a scary risk to take. It's called "living by faith," whether I live in Chicago . . . or even if I move someday to a little house with a wooden porch that overlooks Route 55 and a few square miles of corn in Odell, Chenoa, Cayuga, or Gillum.

—Gary Wilde

▶ GOD ENTERS THE STORY

Do not let your hearts be troubled. Trust in God; trust also in Me. In My Father's house are many rooms; if it were not so, I would have told you. I am going there to prepare a place for you. And if I go and prepare a place for you, I will come back and take you to be with Me that you also may be where I am. You know the way to the place where I am going.

—*John 14:1-4*

Now we know that if the earthly tent we live in is destroyed, we have a building from God, an eternal house in heaven, not built by human hands. Meanwhile we groan, longing to be clothed with our heavenly dwelling, because when we are clothed, we will not be found naked.

For while we are in this tent, we groan and are burdened, because we do not wish to be unclothed but to be clothed with our heavenly dwelling, so that what is mortal may be swallowed up by life. Now it is God who has made us for this very purpose and has given us the Spirit as a deposit, guaranteeing what is to come.

—*2 Corinthians 5:1-5*

Our citizenship is in heaven.
—*Philippians 3:20*

▶ THE STORY IN QUOTES

This is the longing of all mankind—to have security, to know where one's place is. God created man and then He created a place for him, the Garden of Eden. When man lost God he lost at the same time his place. Since then, the longing for a place where he belongs, where he feels at home, is in the heart of every human being. In light of this, Jesus' promise "to prepare a place" for us is filled with new meaning. Those who have found Him have found their place.

—Walter Trobisch[13]

Our society has inundated us with the importance of importance. We have been conditioned to believe in the big, the fast, the expensive, and the far away. I'm still convinced that if you have to move even ten inches from where you are now in order to be happy, you never will be. Life becomes precious and more special to us when we look for the little everyday miracles and get excited again about the privilege of simply being human.

—Tim Hansel[14]

► CAN YOU RELATE?

► Which one of the three story-sections above "rang a bell" with you? In what ways?

► What personal story or experience comes to mind, in relation to these themes:

(a) wanting to create a carefree life

(b) longing for security and settledness

► What other insights came to the surface for you? What questions were raised in your mind? What personal applications are you considering?

► What else would you like to say about this topic?

▶ FOR FURTHER THOUGHT OR DISCUSSION

▶ Have you ever been to a place that you felt was "heavenly"? Tell about that.

▶ Many men secretly believe they can create the perfect situation or environment for themselves and their families. They are thus constantly harried with the "fix-ups" that this requires them to perform—on machines or on the personalities in their families. In what ways would you say that you try to make your life on earth "perfect"? How well have you been able to do that?

▶ Does God really promise us continual bliss in settled happiness? Should we direct all our energies toward trying to produce that state? Or can we learn to be content, even in the midst of daily "chaos"? Explain.

▶ How do you, personally, handle the longings and frustrations of "not being Home yet"?

▶ Is the promise of heaven an encouragement to you (to keep growing as a Christian)? If so, how?

▶ PRAYER MOMENTS

Spend some time going around the circle, naming specific prayer needs. Use the Prayer Record *on page 62 to jot notes. Then, choose a prayer method below.*

__ One man prays, covering issues and concerns raised.

__ Everyone prays for the man on his right.

__ Pray sentence prayers, with a person designated to close.

___ Focus on one key concern of the group or a group member, and all pray about that concern.

___ Spend some moments in silent prayer.

___ Assign specific prayer subjects to people before bowing for prayer.

___ Lay hands on a brother who expresses need, and focus on that man's situation.

___ Sing the doxology, or a praise chorus.

___ Other method:

▶ SUGGESTION FOR THE WEEK AHEAD

During a Quiet Time this week, direct your attention to this phrase in Tim Hansel's quote: "If you have to move even ten inches from where you are now in order to be happy, you never will be."

Chart your family's moves (with dates, places, reasons for the move, and level of resulting happiness) over the years. Ask yourself: *Which moves were likely according to the will of God? Were any of the moves undertaken because of boredom, restlessness, envy, status-seeking, or other questionable motives? How has God worked within all the moves to help me grow spiritually?*

Serving...
Here and Now

What's happening with you?

- ▶ A feeling to report
- ▶ A problem to share
- ▶ A personal or spiritual growth question or insight
- ▶ A summary of your week: issues, concerns, and joys
- ▶ A progress report or accountability check

▶ ONE MAN'S STORY

The first time he came to the door, I didn't recognize him. With his dirty Levis and white stubble, I thought he was homeless. But why here? Eight miles from town? On a gravel road? Then I remembered the bushy eyebrows, the crooked jaw, the way he was dressed when my father introduced him to me as one of the last true cowboys.

"Hi, Jack," I said, and he grinned a yellow grin.

After that, he never called. He just showed up. And since I worked out of the house as a writer, there was no escape.

Not that Jack wasn't interesting. After all, he emigrated from Ireland in his teens, and rode the Rocky Mountain range as a cowboy. To this day, he plays the fiddle and the tin whistle and writes ballads about the Old West. But he also desperately needs attention. So there is no conversation with Jack. Only monologues. After he is in the door, everyone becomes a captive audience.

Once, when I heard knocking, I was particularly frustrated. All morning my plans had been thrown off. I took my time finishing the paragraph I was writing, and when I looked out the window, Jack was already halfway to his pickup. He had taken off his cowboy hat, and white wisps of hair swirled on his balding head, giving him a fragile appearance. He hesitated, and I shrank from the window. I thought about going to the door and calling out, but I didn't. Instead, I waited as he turned the pickup in the driveway.

As Jack drove away that day, his dog lay in the bed of the truck, staring back at me with its one good eye. I had the urge to swear at it. "Come on, I'm not that bad. I have work to do. Would a banker drop everything if Jack showed up at the office? Would a doctor stop treating patients?" Later, though, when I opened the door to get my son from child-care, I nearly stepped on a loaf of bread. As always, Jack had brought some day-old bread he got at a discount from the grocery store.

I picked up the bread and held it, a symbol of Jack — old, but oddly generous. And I felt rebuffed. He had brought me something, but he had gotten nothing in return.

—Tim Bascom

▶ GOD ENTERS THE STORY

He wanted to justify himself, so he asked Jesus, "And who is my neighbor?" In reply Jesus said: "A man was going down from Jerusalem to Jericho, when he fell into the hands of robbers. They stripped him of his clothes, beat him and went away, leaving him half dead. A priest happened to be going down the same road, and when he saw the man, he passed by on the other side. So too, a Levite, when he came to the place and saw him, passed by on the other side.

"But a Samaritan, as he traveled, came where the man was; and when he saw him, he took pity on him. He went to him and bandaged his wounds, pouring on oil and wine. Then he put the man on his own donkey, took him to an inn and took care of him.

"The next day he took out two silver coins and gave them to the innkeeper. 'Look after him,' he said, 'and when I return, I will reimburse you for any extra expense you may have.'

"Which of these three do you think was a neighbor to the man who fell into the hands of robbers?"

The expert in the law replied, "The one who had mercy on him." Jesus told him, "Go and do likewise."

—*Luke 10:29-37*

Then the King will say to those on His right, "Come, you who are blessed by My Father; take your inheritance, the kingdom prepared for you since the creation of the world. For I was hungry and you gave Me something to eat, I was thirsty and you gave Me something to drink, I was a

stranger and you invited Me in, I needed clothes and you clothed Me, I was sick and you looked after Me, I was in prison and you came to visit Me."
— *Matthew 25:34-36*

My command is this: Love each other as I have loved you. Greater love has no one than this, that he lay down his life for his friends.
— *John 15:12-13*

▶ THE STORY IN QUOTES

Stop regarding all the unpleasant things as interruptions of [your] "own," or "real" life. The truth is of course that what one calls the interruptions are precisely one's real life — the life God is sending one day by day.
— C.S. Lewis[15]

It is not enough merely to exist. It's not enough to say, "I'm earning enough to support my family, I do my work well. I'm a good father, husband, churchgoer." That's all very well. But you must do something more. Seek always to do some good, somewhere. Every man has to seek in his own way to realize his true worth. You must give some time to your fellow man. Even if it's a little thing, do something for those who need help, something for which you get no pay but the privilege of doing it. For remember, you don't live in a world all your own. Your brothers are here too.
— Albert Schweitzer[16]

The average American today suffers no twinge of conscience when he passes the sick man on the road.

He knows he has paid the "Good Samaritan" to come along after him and take care of this rather unpleasant social obligation. But the import of Christ's teaching is very plain. He expects us to take the role of the Good Samaritan, and not delegate our Christian love and compassion and concern in every instance to a paid professional or functionary. We are enjoined to love our neighbor—not just to pay taxes to employ someone else to love our neighbor.

—John B. Anderson[17]

▶ CAN YOU RELATE?

▶ Which one of the three story-sections above "rang a bell" with you? How?

▶ What personal story or experience comes to mind, in relation to these themes:

(a) being "under siege" by an unwanted visitor

(b) finding the balance between self-preservation and compassionate outreach

▶ What other insights came to the surface for you? What questions were raised in your mind? What personal applications are you considering?

▶ What else would you like to say about this topic?

▶ FOR FURTHER THOUGHT OR DISCUSSION

▶ How do you typically respond to a person in need?

▶ What is your experience with people who "desperately need attention," as Cowboy Jack did?

▶ How have you arranged your priorities—especially financial—in order to care for the hurting people in the world? How have you reached out in

love to your neighbor who needs Christ?
► Is it easier, or harder, to help someone who is physically "messed up" (as in Luke 10) than to help someone who is emotionally "messed up"?

► PRAYER MOMENTS

Spend some time going around the circle, naming specific prayer needs. Use the Prayer Record *on page 62 to jot notes. Then, choose a prayer method below.*

__ One man prays, covering issues and concerns raised.
__ Everyone prays for the man on his right.
__ Pray sentence prayers, with a person designated to close.
__ Focus on one key concern of the group or a group member, and all pray about that concern.
__ Spend some moments in silent prayer.
__ Assign specific prayer subjects to people before bowing for prayer.
__ Lay hands on a brother who expresses need, and focus on that man's situation.
__ Sing the doxology, or a praise chorus.

► SUGGESTION FOR THE WEEK AHEAD

For one whole day, or more, try keeping a record of your activities, being especially alert to interruptions.
Take time later to evaluate your record. Think: *What typical interruptions in my daily life are actually "opportunities in disguise" for ministry?*

Group
Strengtheners

Draw on the following resources to deepen the fellowship in your group, both in the meeting and during the week.

CREATIVE SESSION STARTERS

Here are some creative ideas to help you launch into the topic of each session. For some sessions you'll just immediately start with discussion, but other times you may want to plan ahead and prepare to use one of these more active starter ideas. A few days in advance, read through the suggestion for your week to see if it would spark interest and discussion in your group. Feel free to adapt the ideas to your own group's size and setting. It's your call!

For Session 1
Start off your session by focusing on the overall theme of the course: living at peace. First ask your group members to find a partner, and then hand

each pair a sheet of paper and a pencil or marker. Tell the men that their task is to fill in a P-E-A-C-E acrostic that describes "the Christian man at peace." For example:

P plans
E effort
A acceptance
C Christ-centered
E expertise

When the pairs are through jotting their acrostics, re-gather everyone and work together to make a "master acrostic" (on chalkboard or newsprint), consisting of the best word ideas from the pairs of men. As the group considers the acrostic, discuss: *What are the greatest roadblocks to peace in a man's life today?*

For Session 2
Distribute an index card and pencil to each man. Say: "Think through your childhood, adolescence, and early adulthood. Make a list of some of the things you were going to be when you grew up." In other words, you are asking the men to list some of the vocational dreams or goals they have had at points in their past. Ask them to arrange their lists in chronological order in order to demonstrate how their plans have changed over the years.

When everyone has a list, ask for the cards, shuffle them, and read them aloud. Have everyone try to guess which card belongs to whom. Ask volunteers to provide more detail about the "success" or "failure" of their vocational plans before you make the transition to today's theme: coping with frustrated dreams.

For Session 3

Hand a sheet of paper and a crayon to each man. Ask group members to diagram a "relational conflict pattern" they sometimes have with their wife. This should be an argument that seems to follow predictable lines of escalation to its inevitable conclusion. Tell the men that they can just symbolize—with a drawing or doodle—how this conflict proceeds. Let them know that they will NOT be asked to share any details of the argument (unless they wish to do so). (Note: Unmarried men could do diagrams that represent family, friendships, or dating relationships.)

Hand out pieces of masking tape and have everyone tape their diagrams to the wall before discussing together: *What is needed to break the kinds of conflict patterns we've displayed?*

For Session 4

Begin the session by announcing that some psychologists say there are only four basic emotions: joy, anger, fear, and sadness (jot them on the chalkboard or newsprint, if possible). Then hand out index cards, which have been prepared in advance with one of the emotion words written on each card. Give one card to each man and say: "In a few moments, be prepared to tell about a time when you were feeling this emotion in a powerful way."

Listen to some of the stories together before moving into your session on the topic of emotional wholeness.

For Session 5

Begin with this thought-starter question: "What was your 'security blanket' when you were a young child?"

Ask the men to recall what they held on to as a child: was it actually an old blanket? a toy? a stuffed animal? a friend? Or did they *not* have a security item?

After some of the men have had a chance to talk about this, hand everyone a sheet of paper and a pencil. Invite the men to write one or two words on the paper that describe what would be written on their adult, present-day "security blanket" (for example: "bank account," "home equity," "job," "parents," "health," "my talents," "my education," etc.).

Ask the men to write something other than "God," something that would be a temptation for them to *replace God with* as the primary locus of security in their lives. Invite volunteers to share what they've written before you move into your session.

For Session 6

Launch your session by having someone read aloud the Parable of the Good Samaritan (page 48). Then give the group a chance to think about a modern-day Good Samaritan scenario they've experienced or witnessed. Ask for sharing about those situations before discussing: *What things make it difficult for a Christian man to be a Good Samaritan today? What makes it rewarding?*

FELLOWSHIP DAY IDEA STARTER

A men's group can be more than just a weekly meeting. For the best results in deepening your fellowship, schedule outside activities at least once per quarter. Try doing a sports activity, or attending a special event together. With a little planning, you can make these outings into times of Christian fellowship.

Recall Session Six's focus on service, and consider emphasizing the fellowship we can have in serving together. Here's what your group could do:

▸ 1. Hold a brainstorming session. Gather ideas for service projects that a group of men could do in the community or within the congregation.

▸ 2. Do some planning. Choose a day and time to meet. Gather equipment needed, and decide who will be in charge of which tasks.

▸ 3. Gather, and do the work together.

▸ 4. Evaluate the activity. At your next meeting, talk about: *What good did we do? What did we learn about one another? What did we learn about Christian service?*

VIDEO NIGHT DISCUSSION OUTLINE

Here's a suggestion for a video to watch with your group at some time during the weeks of your study. You may wish to use the video night as a way of launching, or you could use it as a post-course get-together. (Warning: This video contains an occasional coarse word. Preview it first to decide if it is appropriate for your particular group.)

Movie: *Field of Dreams*
  ▸ PG
  ▸ 106 minutes
  ▸ A 1989 film

What's It All About?

Field of Dreams is a fantasy-drama about baseball, pursuing a dream, and mending a relationship with a father. Though the film borders on the thoroughly unbelievable (with a "voice" talking from a cornfield, old baseball players walking in and out of a center-field "heaven," and time travel back to a town in 1972), it somehow gets us to suspend disbelief because of its thematic realism. It taps into themes of longing for fulfillment and of a father-son relationship that transcends the "magical" elements that might make the film, otherwise, seem silly. Perhaps we recognize early on that much of the action is intended to be allegorical or symbolic.

Christians will immediately realize that the "theology" of the film, while wonderfully sentimental and filled with religious symbolism, comes nowhere near a portrayal of Christian orthodoxy. Nevertheless, viewers may well appreciate the film's ability to accurately and powerfully name the struggles that men feel in pursuing their dreams and wanting their father's blessing.

The Main Characters

- ▶ Ray Kinsella: a former hippie, now living with his wife and daughter on a farm in Iowa
- ▶ Annie Kinsella: Ray's wife
- ▶ John Kinsella: Ray's father
- ▶ "Shoeless Joe" Jackson: star baseball player for the Chicago White Sox in the early 1900s
- ▶ Terrence Mann: a retired civil rights activist and writer
- ▶ Archibald Walker: a doctor who once played a half-inning of professional baseball

The Plot in a Nutshell

Standing in his cornfield, Ray Kinsella hears a voice whispering, "If you build it, he will come." Ray comes to understand that he must plow under part of his crop to build a ball field, allowing "Shoeless Joe" Jackson (who was banned from the game at the height of his career)—and others—to come back and play the game. It is a great risk for Ray to consider, since he is on the verge of losing his farm. Building and maintaining the field will mean bankruptcy. Nevertheless, he takes a leap of faith, and magically, not only does Joe return, but Ray's own father comes back too—as a young ball player.

Discuss:

What does it cost to pursue a dream? Can a relationship with a dead father ever be healed? Can sports help people recognize their deeper longings—for heroes, perfection, even heaven?

Key Themes: Scenes and Quotes

Your discussion may develop more specifically around any of these numbered themes:

▶ 1. *The cost and risk of pursuing a dream.* Early in the film, Ray questions whether he should launch out on the risky project of the ball field.

Ray: "I'm 36 years old. I have a wife, a child, and a mortgage, and I'm scared to death I'm turning into my father."

Annie: "What's your father got to do with all this?"

Ray: "I never forgave him for getting old. By the time he was as old as I am now, he was ancient. He must have had dreams, but he never did anything about them. Dad never did one spontaneous thing in all the years I knew him."

Discuss:

When have you had to take a risk in order to pursue a dream? What benefits and dangers are there in "being spontaneous" in life? Where do you draw the line between prudent planning and "going for it"? Can you give an example?

▶ 2. **The possibility for regret in the remembrance of lost opportunities.** Doc Graham recalls his decision to leave professional baseball, after playing only half an inning, in order to pursue a career in medicine. Ray questions him as to whether Doc has regrets about his decision fifty years later.

Doc: "It was like coming this close to your dreams and then watching them brush past you like a stranger in a crowd. . . . At the time you don't think much of it. You know, we just don't recognize the most significant moments of our lives while they're happening. Back then I thought: 'Well, there will be other days.' I didn't realize . . . that was the only day."

Ray: "Fifty years ago you came so close. I mean, it would kill some men to get that close to their dream and not touch it. They'd consider it a tragedy."

Doc: "Son, if I'd only gotten to be a doctor for half an inning, now that would have been a tragedy."

Discuss:

Do you have regrets about any past decisions you've made? Does God redeem our lost opportunities, or even our "bad" decisions? How?

▶ 3. *The nature of guidance and living by faith.* In the closing credits, "the Voice" is listed as being played by "Himself." Obviously, the Voice is intended to be a portrayal of divine guidance.

Discuss:
Is the Voice a good or poor characterization of God, in your opinion? What insights can a Christian glean about the nature of guidance from Ray's struggles to follow his dream and still provide for his family? Does God tell us exactly what He wants first, then we decide whether to obey or not? Or is it less clear-cut than that in your experience?

▶ 4. *The nature of human longing (for heaven).* Toward the end of the film, Ray and his father, John, meet.

John: "Can I ask you something? . . . Is this heaven?"
Ray: "It's Iowa."
John: "Iowa?"
Ray: "Yeah."
John: "I could have sworn it was heaven."
Ray: "Is there a heaven?"
John: "Oh yeah. It's the place dreams come true."

Discuss:
What "dreams" do all people seem to have? In what sense could we say that heaven is the place where our dreams come true? What might you add to this scene if you were going to make it a clearer statement of biblical truth about heaven?

▶ 5. *Recovering from imperfect fathers.* John Kinsella wanted his son Ray to become a baseball player, but Ray left the sport and left home at seventeen—returning only for his father's funeral.

Terrence: "What happened to your father?"

Ray: "He never made it as a ball player, so he tried to get his son to make it for him. By the time I was ten, playing baseball got to be like eating vegetables or taking out the garbage. So when I was fourteen, I started to refuse. Can you believe that? An American boy refusing to play catch with his father?"

Yet, in the closing scene, we see Ray and his father playing catch together.

Discuss:

Did you play catch with your father? Why is this simple scene so powerful? What is it about Ray and John playing catch that makes it the appropriate closing scene? How does this scene pull everything together in the movie?

PRAYER RECORD

Spend some time sharing prayer concerns before closing your session in prayer. Use this page to jot notes as others speak, then determine together the method you'll use to pray. Periodically review the record as a group to discover how prayers have been answered—or to receive updated information.

Name	Request/Concern/Praise

1. Reprinted from *Dad the Family Coach,* by Dave Simmons (Wheaton, Ill.: Victor Books, 1991). Used by permission.

2. Michael Gurian, *The Prince and the King* (New York: G.P. Putnam's Sons, 1992).

3. Julian Lennon, quoted in *Chicago Tribune,* March 21, 1982.

4. Robin Williams, quoted in Daniel Moore, ed., *Warrior Wisdom* (Philadelphia: Running Press, 1993).

5. Billy Crystal, as Mitch, in the movie *City Slickers.*

6. P.G. Wodehouse, *The Golf Omnibus,* 1973, quoted in *The Oxford Book of Ages* (Oxford: Oxford University Press, 1985).

7. Lloyd Cory, ed., *Quote, Unquote* (Wheaton, Ill.: Scripture Press, 1977).

8. James E. Dittes, *The Male Predicament: On Being a Man Today* (San Francisco: Harper and Row, 1985).

9. Garrison Keillor, *The Book of Guys* (New York: Viking Press, 1993).

10. Stephen Arterburn and David Stoop, *The Angry Man* (Dallas: Word, 1991).

11. Cecil Osborne, *Understanding Your Past* (Millbrae, Calif.: Yokefellow Press, 1980).

12. Robert Bly, "Male Naiveté and the Loss of the Kingdom," in Christopher Harding, ed., *Wingspan: Inside the Men's Movement* (New York: St. Martin's Press, 1992).

13. Walter Trobisch, quoted in *Men's Devotional Bible* (Grand Rapids: Zondervan, 1993).

14. Tim Hansel, quoted in "Points to Ponder," *Reader's Digest*, Dec. 1992.

15. C.S. Lewis, in a letter to Arthur Greeves.

16. Albert Schweitzer, quoted in "Points to Ponder," *Reader's Digest*, Dec. 1992.

17. John B. Anderson, *Between Two Worlds* (Grand Rapids: Zondervan, 1970).